SKI

A MISCELLANY

Compiled by Julia Skinner

With particular reference to the work of Winston Kime

THE FRANCIS FRITH COLLECTION

www.francisfrith.com

First published in the United Kingdom in 2010 by The Francis Frith Collection®

This edition published exclusively for Identity Books in 2010 ISBN 978-1-84589-517-4

Text and Design copyright The Francis Frith Collection®
Photographs copyright The Francis Frith Collection® except where indicated.

The Frith® photographs and the Frith® logo are reproduced under licence from
Heritage Photographic Resources Ltd, the owners of the Frith® archive and trademarks.
'The Francis Frith Collection', 'Francis Frith' and 'Frith' are registered trademarks of
Heritage Photographic Resources Ltd.

All rights reserved. No photograph in this publication may be sold to a third party other than in the original
form of this publication, or framed for sale to a third party. No parts of this publication may be reproduced,
stored in a retrieval system, or transmitted, in any form, or by any means, electronic, mechanical, photocopying,
recording or otherwise, without the prior permission of the publishers and copyright holder.

British Library Cataloguing in Publication Data

Did You Know? Skegness - A Miscellany
Compiled by Julia Skinner
With particular reference to the work of Winston Kime

The Francis Frith Collection
Frith's Barn, Teffont,
Salisbury, Wiltshire SP3 5QP
Tel: +44 (0) 1722 716 376
Email: info@francisfrith.co.uk
www.francisfrith.com

Printed and bound in Malaysia

Front Cover: **SKEGNESS, SOUTH PARADE 1899** 44346p

The colour-tinting is for illustrative purposes only, and is not intended to be historically accurate

AS WITH ANY HISTORICAL DATABASE, THE FRANCIS FRITH ARCHIVE IS CONSTANTLY BEING
CORRECTED AND IMPROVED, AND THE PUBLISHERS WOULD WELCOME INFORMATION ON
OMISSIONS OR INACCURACIES

CONTENTS

- 4   Introduction
- 6   Lincolnshire Words and Phrases
- 8   Haunted Skegness
- 12   Skegness Miscellany
- 40   Sporting Skegness
- 44   Quiz Questions
- 46   Recipes
- 50   Quiz Answers
- 54   Francis Frith - Pioneer Victorian Photographer

Did You Know?
SKEGNESS
A MISCELLANY

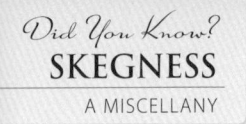

SKEGNESS, FROM THE PIER 1910 62844

Did You Know?
SKEGNESS
A MISCELLANY

Did You Know?
SKEGNESS
A MISCELLANY

INTRODUCTION

'The great charm of Skegness is undoubtedly in its shore of clean and hard sand which stretches north and south in an unbroken line for miles. At low water a large tract of land is laid bare, and here, as the tide gradually ebbs out 'young Englanders' can wade in the shallow creeks right to low water mark. These sands are indeed a very paradise for children, as they are free from the dangers inseparable from places where there are lofty cliffs, which will of necessity entail anxiety where there are young ones.'

From 'Skegness and Neighbourhood: A Handbook for Visitors' by E A Jackson (1883)

Skegness – or Skeggy, as it is affectionately known by those who love it – owed its popular success as a seaside resort to the railway, which reached here in 1873 as an extension from the then terminus at Wainfleet. There had already been a middle-class watering place here, attached to what was little more than a fishing village, but a new town was laid out from 1876 by the Earl of Scarbrough, and in 1881 the new resort of Skegness acquired a splendid pier, seen in photograph 51763 (page 28) and unrecognisable to the modern visitor.

Skegness was famously promoted in the early 20th century by a railway poster bearing the slogan 'Skegness is so bracing'. Bracing is a good word to describe the north and east winds that frequently blow onto the coast here, but the wide sandy beaches are superb compensation. Skegness was very much developed with day trips and excursions in mind, utilising the railway, and was especially popular with visitors from the industrial towns of the Midlands. In photograph 62843 (opposite) we can see the funfair actually on the sands above the high water mark, including a helter-skelter tower.

Did You Know?
SKEGNESS
A MISCELLANY

Skegness has lost nothing of its attraction for visitors in recent years, and was described in the 'Lonely Planet' guide to Great Britain as 'everything you would want' in a seaside resort – just what the Earl of Scarbrough hoped that his 'New Skegness' would be, when he planned it back in the 1870s.

SKEGNESS, FROM THE PIER 1910   62843

LINCOLNSHIRE DIALECT WORDS AND PHRASES

'Chunter' – to complain.

'Frim folk' – people from other areas.

'Gimmer' – a ewe (female sheep) which has never given birth.

'Jiffle' – fidget.

'Kecks' – trousers.

'Kelch' – mud.

'Mardy' – bad tempered, sulky.

'Proggle' – to poke about (with a stick).

'Reasty' – rancid.

'Starnil' – a starling.

'Throng' – busy.

'Uneppen' – clumsy.

'Wassack' or *'Gump'* – a fool.

'Wick' – lively.

'Yellowbelly' – a term for a Lincolnshire person. There are many theories about the origin of the name, but one of the favourite explanations is that it derives from the bright yellow waistcoat which was worn by the 10th Regiment of Foot, later The Lincolnshire Regiment.

'Yucker' – a young person.

On *'Mumping Day'* – or St Thomas's Day, 21st December – it was the custom in Lincolnshire for poor people to go around begging for Christmas fare.

SKEGNESS, LUMLEY ROAD 1910 62855

Did You Know?
SKEGNESS
A MISCELLANY

HAUNTED SKEGNESS

In former centuries the coast around Skegness was the domain of smugglers. One of their favourite inns was the Vine Inn in Vine Road, believed to be the second oldest building in the town and now trading as the Best Western Vine Hotel. The ghost of a man wearing old-fashioned clothes is said to wander the corridors of the hotel, and sightings of him have also been reported in one of the hotel bedrooms. Legend says that this is the ghost of a customs and excise officer from Boston who was murdered by smugglers in the early 19th century, and whose body was bricked up in a cell in the hotel walls. When building work was being done on the hotel in 1902, the skeleton of a man was found; the remains were dressed in uniform, complete with brass buttons bearing the royal crest, and presumably this was the unfortunate revenue officer, who was last seen alive in the Vine Inn.

In the 1970s several pupils at Skegness Grammar School reported seeing a ghostly figure, resembling a monk wearing a brown habit, in the corridor by the school's assembly hall. The school caretaker at the time also reported seeing the mysterious figure.

A famous ghost story from the Skegness area is linked with Gunby Hall, seven miles west of the town, off the A158. The hall is said to be haunted by two ghosts, although the event which inspired the ghost story actually occurred at Bratoft Castle, which used to stand nearby. The story goes that in the late 17th century a young woman called Margaret, the daughter of Sir William Massingberd of Bratoft Castle, fell in love with one of her father's servants. When Sir William discovered their affair he shot the man dead. In 1698, filled with remorse for his act, Sir William had Bratoft Castle demolished and then built Gunby Hall to live in. The ghost of his daughter and her doomed lover are said to wander along the path beside the pond near Gunby Hall, which is now known as the Ghost Walk.

Did You Know?
SKEGNESS
A MISCELLANY

SKEGNESS, NORTH SHORE c1955 S134032

Did You Know?
SKEGNESS
A MISCELLANY

**SKEGNESS, THE PADDLING POOL
c1955** S134036

Did You Know?
SKEGNESS
A MISCELLANY

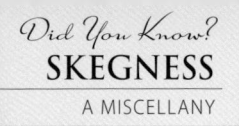

SKEGNESS MISCELLANY

Skegness is much older than the Domesday Book, compiled in 1086. The name of the town derives from the time when this part of England was settled and controlled by the Danes, or Vikings, but it was a haven town even earlier, in Roman times. The Skegness that was known to the Romans and Vikings was swept away by the tide in 1526 and lies under the sea perhaps three-quarters of a mile from the present shore.

The ancient Norse heritage of Lincolnshire from when the area was under Danish (or Viking) control is still evident today in many of the county's place-names, especially those ending in '-by', '-toft', '-thorpe', and '-ness', meaning respectively 'town' or 'village', 'homestead', 'hamlet', and 'headland' – as at Skegness.

SKEGNESS, LUMLEY ROAD 1899 44192

SKEGNESS, GRAND PARADE 1899 44348

In 1801 the rebuilt village of Skegness had a population of only 134, with a further 221 in the adjoining parish of Winthorpe. The inhabitants gained a living grazing sheep and cattle on the rich pastures of the marsh, between the Wolds, and there were a few inshore fishermen.

The fashion for sea bathing began to catch on in Skegness around the turn of the 18th and 19th centuries. Sea bathing was restricted almost entirely to the wealthier classes, who had taken up the fashion for the seaside which had been set by royalty on the south coast. The Lincolnshire squires drove to Skegness, Mablethorpe and Freiston Shore to keep in the swing. The Skegness Inn (later the Vine Hotel) and the New Inn (Hildreds Hotel) and a number of lodging houses catered for the visitors, but it was only when the railway arrived in 1873 that the sea rather than the surrounding green fields provided the local villagers' main source of income.

Did You Know?
SKEGNESS
A MISCELLANY

After the railway arrived in 1873 the Great Northern Railway began running Sunday excursions from the towns and cities of the East Midlands, and Skegness struggled to cope with the boisterous hordes that thronged the High Street on their way to the shore. There was nothing at Skegness but the sands and the sea and the invigorating air, and the village was hard put to feed the multitude and keep them out of mischief. Almost all the land and farm holdings in Skegness belonged to the Earl of Scarbrough, who resided at Sandbeck Park near Rotherham. In the 1870s agriculture was going through a difficult time, and with the coming of the railway Lord Scarbrough decided to develop Skegness as a model watering place. Although this would be an expensive project, the long-term prospect appeared to make it a sound investment. Work began in 1877, and the next five years saw the tiny coastal village overlaid with wide tree-lined avenues, a new main street, promenades and villas, homes and lodging houses to suit all classes. New residents began pouring in to the town to open businesses or work on the construction.

SKEGNESS, LUMLEY ROAD c1955 S134092

SKEGNESS, GRAND PARADE 1910 62845

Even before the new streets of the Earl of Scarbrough's development plans for Skegness were laid out, the Earl's agent, Henry Tippet, concentrated the main building gang on a stone wall parallel with the seashore, forming a last line of defence but primarily intended to be a retaining wall for the building of the promenade. Limestone blocks were brought by rail from Roche Abbey quarry, which was owned by Lord Scarbrough and situated near Sandbeck Park, his South Yorkshire residence. The wall ran from the north end of the town as far south as Derby Avenue, although the parades never stretched the full extent of the wall at either end. The promenade was protected by robust iron railing with wide footpaths and carriageways, and the land side was quickly built up with lodging house on the Grand and South Parades. The extension of Lumley Road across the parade leading to the foreshore was called the Lumley Pullover, which was later to be Tower Pullover, and finally Tower Esplanade.

Did You Know?
SKEGNESS
A MISCELLANY

Photograph 51770 (below) shows Lumley Avenue with its chestnut trees and wide verges and roadway, typical of the streets comprising the original grid layout of the Earl of Scarbrough's 1870s town plan. The parish church stands in Powletts Circus at the far end.

Lumley Avenue, Lumley Road and Lumley Square were so-named after the Earl of Scarbrough's family name. Photograph 44354 (opposite) shows Lumley Road in 1899. This view is utterly transformed now from Roman Bank, a reference to the old Roman sea wall. The charming rustic stone lion on the roof above the corner entrance of the Lion Hotel on the extreme left of this view has now been replaced by a corner turret (see item on page 17), and all the buildings are now shops, many of which have been rebuilt. However, the view is still terminated by the Jubilee Clock Tower.

SKEGNESS, LUMLEY AVENUE 1904 51770

SKEGNESS, LUMLEY ROAD 1899 44354

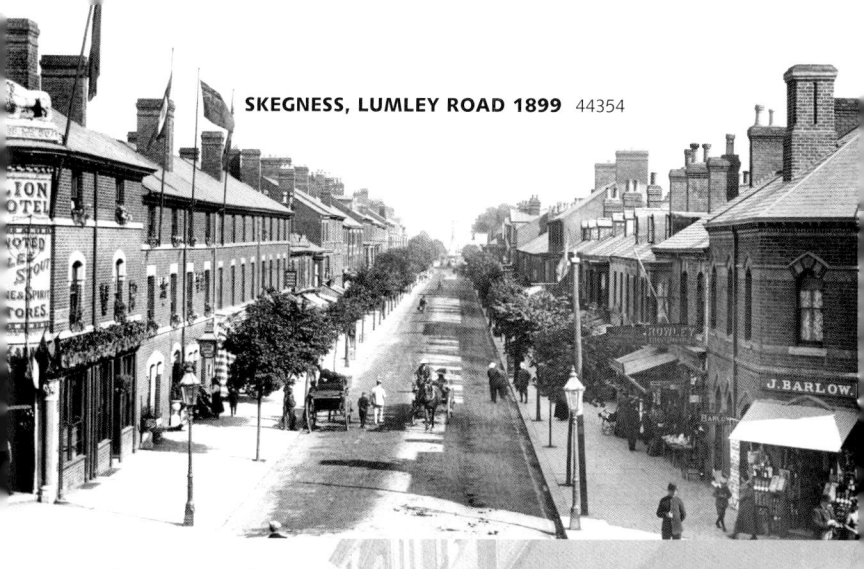

The Lion Hotel in Lumley Road opened in 1881. A unique feature of the new hotel was the stone lion perched on the roof above the corner entrance (seen in photograph 44354, above). It was carved from sandstone by Richard Winn of Grimsby (1823-1912). The stone lion was conveyed the forty-odd miles from Grimsby on a horse-drawn dray. It eventually became unsafe on the roof, and in 1904 it was brought down to stand on the pavement on the Roman Bank frontage. There it remained almost throughout the 20th century, to the great delight of thousands of small children who could never pass that point without demanding 'a ride on the lion'. There is a story that one Saturday night at closing time, a party of young rugby players, in joyful spirits after an evening's celebrations, manhandled the six-hundredweight lion across the road to deposit it outside the Lumley Hotel. Residents passing the Lumley next morning could hardly believe their eyes when they saw the familiar lion guarding the portals of the rival establishment. This much loved emblem disappeared very suddenly shortly before Wetherspoon took over the Lion Hotel in 1997 when, for some undisclosed reason, the new owners decided to rename the hotel the Red Lion.

Did You Know?
SKEGNESS
A MISCELLANY

SKEGNESS, FROM THE BEACH 1899 44201

One of the people who came to live in the newly-developed Skegness was Richard Hudson, who moved here with his wife and children in 1878. The Hudson family lived at the conical-roofed Pier View on the corner of what was once Pier Terrace, seen in the centre of photograph 44201 (above). Richard Hudson and his forebears were already well-known musicians in his native Preston, and he soon opened a music shop in the High Street. He also formed a band and an orchestra to play on the pier. One of his sons, George Hudson, established himself as a maker of fine violins, violas and violincellos, which are now collectors' items. Most of these instruments were made at Pier View, which was trademarked as 'The Cremona Workshop'.

Another musician who worked in Skegness, playing his trombone in the pier orchestra, was the English composer Gustav Holst, born in Cheltenham in 1874. It is recorded that 'he scored his Cotswold Symphony in his free time on the sands' whilst he was living and working in the town.

Did You Know?
SKEGNESS
A MISCELLANY

Pleasure gardens were fashionable at seaside resorts, and were prominent on the Earl of Scarbrough's town plan for Skegness. The ground chosen for the gardens, close to the foreshore, had formerly been a coalyard at a time when small colliers, or 'billyboys', from the Tyne dumped their cargoes on the sands, to be carted away from there. In the summer of 1841 'upwards of 6,000 tons of coal were landed', according to White's Lincolnshire Directory of 1842. The Pleasure Gardens had lawns and flowerbeds, rustic arbours and a pond, and also a bandstand and a large refreshment pavilion, as well as ornamental kiosks at both main entrances. There were also turnstiles where patrons had to pay their pennies for admittance. The Pleasure Gardens were renamed the Tower Gardens in the 1920s.

SKEGNESS, PLEASURE GARDENS 1910 62857

Did You Know?
SKEGNESS
A MISCELLANY

SKEGNESS, THE BEACH 1910 62867

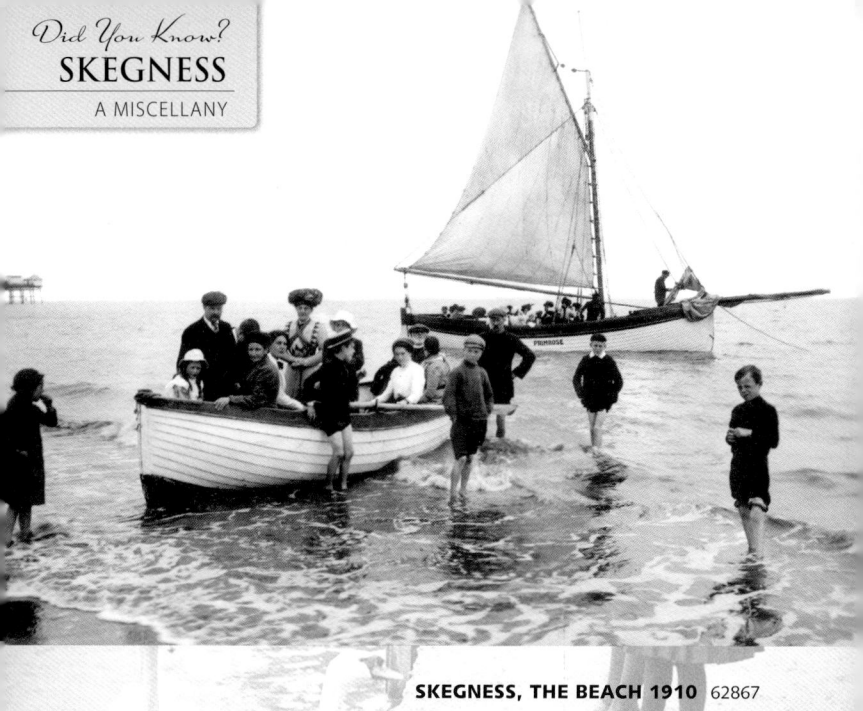

When visitors came to the newly-developed resort of Skegness they found plenty to keep them entertained. On the sands, the fairground was fairly humming with swings and roundabouts, a helter-skelter and a rifle-range, a photo studio, shellfish barrows, pierrot entertainers and bathing machines and, of course, donkeys. In the shallow water, numerous rowing and sailing boats awaited passengers whilst boatmen, in nave guernseys and peaked caps, touted for trips in the 'Primrose' and the 'Shamrock' and other small craft; the seal banks in the Wash were a favourite destination for a boat trip, where hundreds of seals could be seen basking on the exposed sandbanks at low tide.

Did You Know?
SKEGNESS
A MISCELLANY

When the tide was out, horses and carts carried passengers wishing to take a trip in a sail boat across the creeks to the sea, and a boatman then assisted them up a portable plank into the waiting boat, as shown in photograph 62868 (below).

SKEGNESS, THE BEACH 1910 62868

Did You Know?
SKEGNESS
A MISCELLANY

The Earl of Scarbrough's 1870s town plan of New Skegness showed a large new church for the town, St Matthew's (photograph 51771, below), replacing St Clement's in the fields (photograph 62863, opposite). By 1880 the nave and south aisle of St Matthew's Church were completed and services were licensed. Another five years elapsed before the building was considered to be complete, and then problems began with ground subsidence, which caused the abandonment of the partly-built tower. The architect's original plan had been for a tower and spire rising to 130 feet, but a small turret with piped bells had to be substituted.

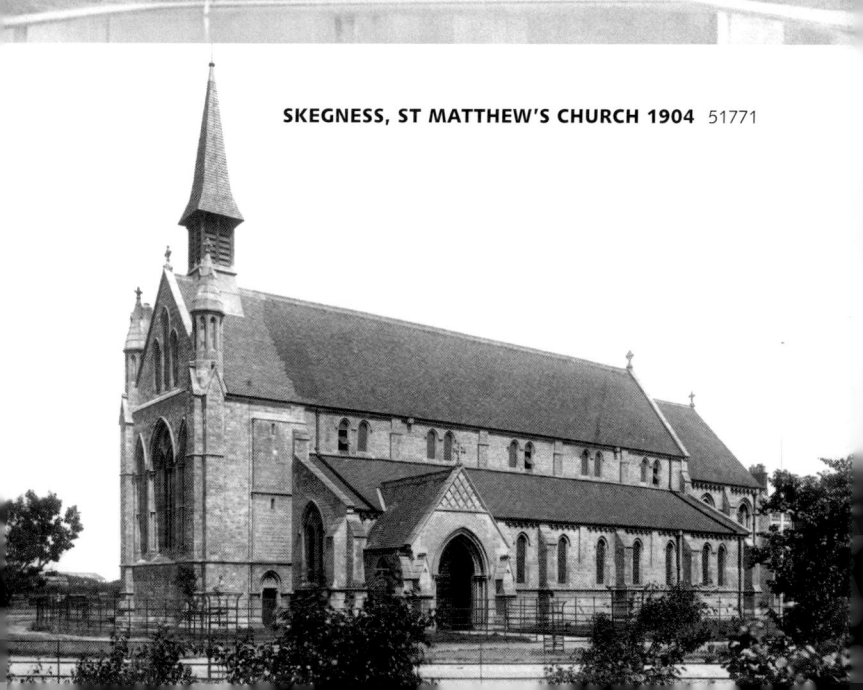

SKEGNESS, ST MATTHEW'S CHURCH 1904 51771

SKEGNESS, ST CLEMENT'S CHURCH 1910 62863

The Primitive Methodists also opened a chapel on Roman Bank in 1899 to accommodate their increasing congregation. However, the Baptists had to wait until 1910 before they had sufficient funds to embark on their present building in Lumley Road, which took the place of their little corrugated iron church. Not far from the Baptists, the Salvation Army raised their Citadel in the High Street in 1929, which was replaced by a new church in 1995. The Roman Catholics built in Grosvenor Road, much earlier, in 1898, and that building served them until the present church was built close by in 1950.

Did You Know?
SKEGNESS
A MISCELLANY

St Mary's Church at Winthorpe is the oldest and the finest of the three Skegness churches, dating from the 15th century, and built on the site of an earlier church (see photograph 26692, below). It was restored in 1881, but the rich carving of the stall-ends in the chancel is a notable feature. The ancient churchyard cross was restored as a war memorial.

SKEGNESS, WINTHORPE CHURCH 1890 26692

SKEGNESS, THE WESLEYAN CHAPEL 1891 29021

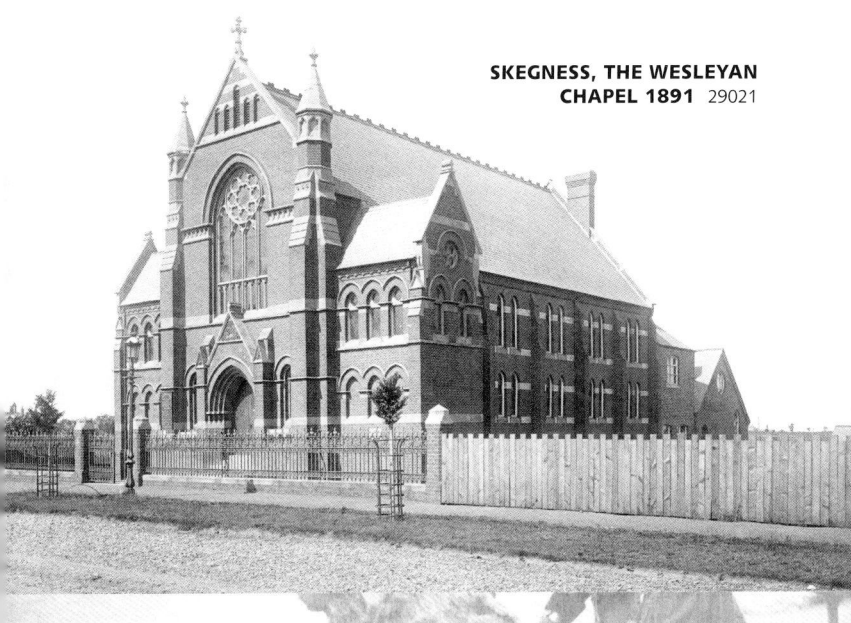

John Wesley, as far as is known, never came nearer to Skegness that Wainfleet, where he preached from the Butter Cross in 1780. His followers, however, are known to have formed a group in the seaside village in about 1820, although it was nearly twenty more years before they were able to build their own little chapel in the narrow main street. The coming of the railway in 1873 brought an increase of members, and the Wesleyan Methodists decided to build a new chapel nearer the west end of the High Street, which was completed in 1876. The building still stands, although it is now a café, and much altered. It had been in use scarcely a year when the Earl of Scarbrough began building the new town, and as the population again expanded it was apparent that the High Street chapel was far too small to seat all the new Wesleyans flocking into the town. The trustees approached the Earl and he generously gave them a new plot in what was to be Algitha Road. Their new place of worship was opened in July 1882, and is shown in photograph 29021, (above). This former Wesleyan Chapel is now the Skegness Methodist Church.

Donkey rides on the beach have long been an essential part of every child's seaside holiday, and this is as true nowadays as it was in 1883 when E A Jackson wrote in his 'Skegness and Neighbourhood: A Handbook for Visitors': 'And then the donkeys! Who can imagine a seaside resort without its herd of gaily caparisoned 'mokes'? Neddy's perennial face appears everywhere, surely nowhere better represented than at Skegness.'

SKEGNESS, DONKEY RIDES c1960 S134110

Did You Know?
SKEGNESS
A MISCELLANY

SKEGNESS, THE PIER 1904 51763

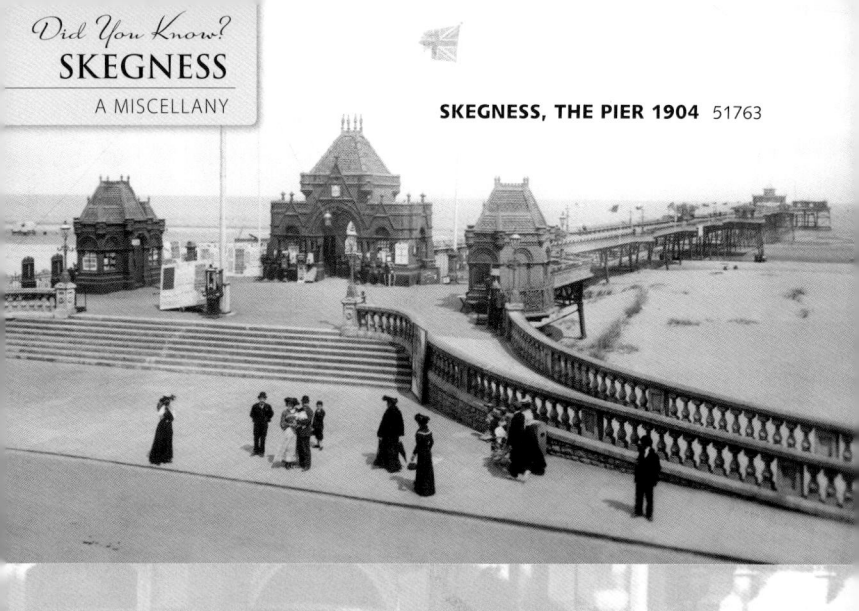

The most dominating structure in Skegness was the pier, which opened in 1881 (photograph 51763, above). Like pleasure gardens, seaside piers were a Victorian creation, but Skegness and Cleethorpes were the only resorts on the Lincolnshire coast to boast such a prestigious amenity. The pier at Cleethorpes had opened eight years earlier, but the Skegness structure was half as long again as its rival's, and at 1,817 feet was claimed to be the fourth longest in the country. The pierhead carried a refreshment saloon and concert stage, whilst the entrance at the land end had a Gothic-style toll-house and trading kiosks. In 1978 the section of the pier between the concert hall and the end was destroyed in storms. The landward end of the 1840-foot-long pier had already been submerged in 1970 by the enclosed Skegness Pier Amusements, although some of the original structure can be seen at the sea end. This view, taken in 1904, shows the resort still in its genteel phase under the Earl of Scarbrough's strict control. It was not until 1921, when the council bought the sea-front and foreshore from the Earl, that the town assumed its brasher kiss-me-quick character.

Did You Know?
SKEGNESS
A MISCELLANY

In 1941, during the Second World War, a bomb fell just in front of Miss Blanchard's Elite Violet Café which had opened beneath the pier in the 1930s, dropped by one of the frequent nuisance raiders that harassed the town during the war. It was lunchtime and so a number of people were inside the café, but luckily for them the bomb buried itself in the sand and did not explode.

Photograph 44353 below shows the sands at low tide in 1899 and the museum ship 'Eliza', which contained a whale skeleton and other marine wonders.

SKEGNESS, THE SANDS 1899 44353

Did You Know?
SKEGNESS
A MISCELLANY

The Jubilee Clock Tower was erected at the junction of Lumley Road with the then seafront's Grand Parade and South Parade. The Tower was built to commemorate Queen Victoria's Diamond Jubilee in 1897; photograph 44195 (opposite) was taken on 11th August 1899, and shows its formal opening by the Countess of Scarbrough.

Lord Scarbrough's Estate Office continued to administer the foreshore of Skegness until after the First World War. The Earl of Scarbrough then decided it was time for him to concentrate his attention on his main interests, agriculture and land ownership. The seaside was no longer to be part of his activities, and in 1921 he offered to sell the whole foreshore to Skegness Urban District Council at the bargain price of £15,000. The town council held a town referendum on the question, but there was never much doubt what the answer would be. As somebody has said, it was the sale of the century.

After the town council took over the running of the foreshore in 1921, there were calls for the attractions of Skegness to be developed to compete with the likes of Cleethorpes. The council's engineer and surveyor, Rowland Jenkins, prepared a foreshore redevelopment scheme converting a large part of the sands and dunes to attractive walks and flower gardens, with a boating lake and bathing pool, a theatre and ballroom, bowling greens and tennis courts, and other features attractive to visitors. The scheme began with the construction of Tower Esplanade, transformed from the old sand pullover. There were a lot of doubters, and the firmest objectors were forecasting that Jenkins' Pier, as it was dubbed, would be washed away by the first spring tides. It seemed they might be right, for the winter gales hurled the water over the partly-constructed esplanade, causing much damage, but this was soon put straight, and when it was completed most people agreed that the new gateway to the sea was big improvement.

SKEGNESS, GRAND PARADE AND THE OFFICIAL OPENING OF THE CLOCK TOWER 1899 44195

Did You Know?
SKEGNESS
A MISCELLANY

31

Did You Know? SKEGNESS A MISCELLANY

For many years the most famous fairground ride at Skegness was the Figure Eight, which was erected at the far end of North Parade in 1908 and was regarded as a worthy rival to Coney Island in the USA. The four-seater cars of the Figure Eight were hauled up the incline by an endless chain, from which point gravity propelled them by hair-raising dips and curves back to ground level. The Figure Eight survived until 1970, when it was dismantled. It has now been replaced by an altogether more testing version as part of the Pleasure Beach complex.

SKEGNESS, THE FIGURE EIGHT 1910 62862

Did You Know?
SKEGNESS
A MISCELLANY

SKEGNESS, THE WATERWAY c1955 S134134

The Waterway took shape in 1931, providing a motorboat service running from the Figure Eight as far as the pier, and seven years later it was extended to Tower Esplanade. Photograph S134134 (above) shows a boat just starting out from the north end of the Waterway, with the Figure Eight switchback, the tennis courts and the 1930s' concrete 'castle ruins' in the background.

33

Did You Know?
SKEGNESS
A MISCELLANY

In 1927 Billy Butlin arrived in Skegness with a couple of living vans and three lorries packed with fairground equipment. He persuaded Lord Scarbrough to rent him a strip of ground on the North Parade frontage of the area known as the Jungle to set up a funfair. (The site is now built over with the County Hotel.) Butlin's mushroom-roofed hoopla stalls were augmented by roundabouts and swingboats, a helter-skelter and eventually a roller coaster. The sea side of North Parade, from the Pier to the Figure Eight, was lined with bowling alleys, a rifle range, race games, the Crystal Maze and an 'aerial flight'. The last-named was an athletic trip for the punter, who was suspended from a steel cable between two raised platforms, with a safety net below for those who did not make the full trip. In 1928 Butlin obtained a long lease from Skegness Council to set up a new funfair on the south side of the pier; the following summer he transferred his stalls and rides there, together with those from across the road, to whom he rented pitches. Butlin retained this big amusement park until 1964, when the tenancy was taken over by Botton Bros, who rebuilt the site from scratch. Billy Butlin eventually retired to Jersey, and died there in 1980. His last visit to Skegness was to switch on the illuminations in 1977, when he stayed at the County Hotel – built on the site of his first Skegness amusement park, which he had established 50 years earlier.

On the left of photograph 62846 (opposite) is the Osbert House Hotel – the name commemorated an earlier Earl of Scarbrough's grandfather. Billy Butlin bought the Osbert House Hotel in the late 1930s and it became Butlin House, head office for all his holiday camps, hotels and amusement parks, which by then were spread across the country. The building was demolished in 1972, to be replaced by the present less imposing cafés and chip shops.

Did You Know?
SKEGNESS
A MISCELLANY

SKEGNESS, GRAND PARADE AND THE CLOCK TOWER 1910 62846

35

SKEGNESS, THE MINERS' WELFARE HOLIDAY CENTRE c1955 S134007

Nottinghamshire and Derbyshire have always had strong ties with Skegness and, at the beginning of the 20th century, both convalescent homes and holiday homes for poor children from those counties were being built here at the seaside. There were special convalescent homes for the coal-mining industry of both counties, and in May 1939 the Derbyshire Miners' Association opened what was then a pioneer venture in the form of a holiday camp solely for the miners and their families. It was situated next to the beach at Seathorne, on Winthorpe Avenue. Different collieries took it in turns to go on holiday en masse to the Skegness camp, so that whole villages would holiday together by the seaside. Over the years the Derbyshire Miners' Welfare Holiday Centre at Seathorne provided happy holidays for thousands of miners and their families until near the end of the 20th century. It was a sad day when the near demise of the coal-mining industry forced its closure and eventual demolition.

Did You Know?
SKEGNESS
A MISCELLANY

Butlin's was not the first holiday camp in the Skegness area, for the Nottingham branch of the YMCA (Young Men's Christian Association) had established a holiday camp in Grosvenor Road in 1920. Accommodation was in bell tents and ex-army huts, but by 1933 these had been replaced by permanent buildings to become the YMCA's Woodside Holiday Centre, eventually open to all comers.

SKEGNESS, THE BATHING POOL c1955 S134033

Did You Know?
SKEGNESS
A MISCELLANY

SKEGNESS, THE PARADE 1899 44346

The great east coast flood of 31st January 1953 saw the tide reaching up to the parade walls and causing immense material damage, but no lives were lost in Skegness and no houses had to be evacuated. However, Butlin's Camp, just outside the town boundary, was completely inundated: the sea reached up to Roman Bank, and six lives were lost there. The sea walls from that point northward to the Humber were swept away, and more than 40 people were drowned.

SPORTING SKEGNESS

There are a number of excellent golf courses and golf links in the Skegness area – but do you know what the difference is between a golf course and a golf links?
– To classify as a links, a course must be within sight of the sea.

Skegness Boating Club is a sea-boating club which is now based at a compound just off the Princes Parade car park. The club had to move its compound from its earlier site after extensive enhancements of the sea defences at Skegness were carried out in the 1990s, when 'rock armour' was installed along Lagoon Walk. This helped to protect the beach at Skegness, but forced higher tides southwards, resulting in the boating club's compound being swamped by the sea.

Skegness Town Association Football Club was established in 1947. The club's nickname is the Lilywhites. Perhaps the most famous footballer to have come from Skegness was the goalkeeper Raymond, or 'Ray', Clemence, born in the town in 1948, who played for Scunthorpe United, Liverpool, Tottenham Hotspur and was capped 61 times for England. He is considered to have been one of England's best-ever goalkeepers, and would probably have played more matches for his country had he not been in competition throughout his career for a place in the national team with Peter Shilton, England's other great goalkeeper of that era.

Skegness Stadium, just outside the town, is a venue for many different types of vehicle racing, including Banger racing, powerful Brisca F1 Stockcar racing, truck racing – and even caravan racing!

THE BOATING LAKE c1955 S134073

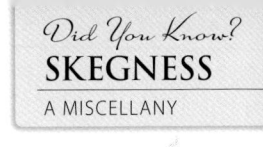

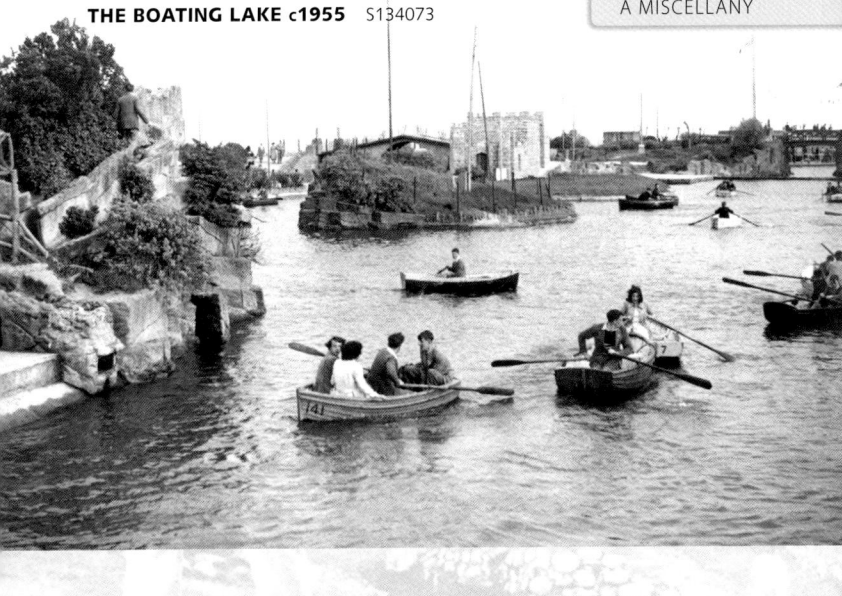

Did You Know?
SKEGNESS
A MISCELLANY

A meeting of rugby enthusiasts at the Links Hotel in 1949 resulted in the formation of the present Skegness Rugby Union Football Club. There had been two short-lived earlier clubs in the town, in the 1920s and 1930s. Since 1987 the club has run a popular and successful veterans' tournament each September, which attracts teams from all over England.

Skegness is also a major centre for bowls, and hosts the high-profile national championships of the English Bowling Federation each year.

Skegness Cricket Club has been in existence since at least 1877 and plays at the Richmond Drive ground, renowned for its excellent facilities. At the end of the 2009 season the club celebrated probably the most successful season in its history, with the first team finishing as runners-up in the Lincolnshire ECB Premier League.

Did You Know?
SKEGNESS
A MISCELLANY

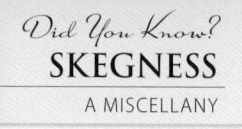

SKEGNESS, THE BEACH 1910 62865

42

Did You Know?
SKEGNESS
A MISCELLANY

43

QUIZ QUESTIONS

Answers on page 50.

1. What is the origin of the name 'Skegness'?

2. Skegness is on the shore of the North Sea – by what name was this sea formerly known?

3. What is the name of the nature reserve south of the town?

4. Skegness has a number of nicknames – how many can you name?

5. Here is a nostalgic one for drivers of a certain age – what is unusual about the 'No Waiting' sign in Lumley Road seen on the left hand side of photograph S134062, opposite?

6. A major exhibition takes place in the Embassy Theatre in Skegness each year featuring which modelmaker's craft?

7. Where in Skegness can you find a boat called the 'Lincolnshire Poacher'?

8. Where in Skegness will you find Bob the traction engine?

9. What April Fool's Day hoax was pulled by the 'Skegness Standard' in 2009?

10. What event in Skegness's history is known as the Battle of Granny's Opening?

SKEGNESS, LUMLEY ROAD c1955 S134062

Did You Know?
SKEGNESS
A MISCELLANY

RECIPE

COCKLES AND BACON

Shellfish stalls selling cockles, mussels, whelks and oysters have long been a feature of Skegness. This recipe makes a tasty snack.

> 600ml/1 pint (volume) fresh cockles
> 8 rashers of streaky bacon
> A little oil or lard for frying
> Bread slices for toast
> Butter

Wash the cockles thoroughly in plenty of cold water, or leave them to soak for several hours if possible.

Bring a large saucepan of water to the boil. Place the pre-soaked cockles in the water and leave for a few minutes, until their shells have opened. Remove from heat, strain and leave the cockles to cool.

When cooled, pick the cockles out of their shells. Fry the bacon rashers in a little oil or lard until they are crisp, then remove from the pan and keep warm. Add the cockles to the pan and toss them in the bacon fat until they are lightly browned. Serve the cockles and bacon on slices of hot buttered toast.

SKEGNESS, THE MODEL YACHT POND c1955 S134064

Did You Know?
SKEGNESS
A MISCELLANY

SKEGNESS, NORTH PARADE c1955 S134043

RECIPE

LINCOLNSHIRE PLUM BREAD

This is especially good if the dried fruit is soaked overnight in cold (milk-less) tea before cooking.

- 450g/1 lb plain flour (strong bread-making flour is best)
- 225g/8oz prunes, cut into small pieces
- 115ml/4fl oz milk, warmed
- 115g/4oz butter, melted
- 4 tablespoonfuls caster sugar
- 50g/2oz currants
- 50g/2oz sultanas
- 15g/ 1/2 oz easy-blend dried yeast
- 2 eggs, lightly beaten
- 1 teaspoonful ground cinnamon
- 1 teaspoonful ground allspice
- 1 pinch of salt

Mix together the warmed milk, sugar, butter, yeast, beaten egg, salt, and spices. Add the flour, and beat the mixture until it is smooth, to make soft pliable dough. Turn out the dough onto a floured surface, and knead it until it is smooth and elastic. Place the dough in a bowl, cover, and allow the bowl to stand in a warm place until the dough has doubled in size. Knock back the dough and knead it again briefly, adding the dried fruit and making sure that it is evenly distributed. Divide the dough into two pieces, and place into two 450g (1 lb) greased and lined loaf tins. Cover and leave again in a warm place rise until doubled in size.

Pre-heat the oven to 190°C/375°F/Gas Mark 5. Place the loaf tins on a pre-heated baking sheet and bake for 40-50 minutes, then remove the loaves from the tins and return them to the oven to cook for a further 5-10 minutes, or until they sound hollow when tapped on the base. Store the loaves in an airtight container and serve in slices, spread with butter. This also makes excellent toast.

QUIZ ANSWERS

1. The name of Skegness comes from the Norse language, and probably means 'Skeggi's headland', named after a Norseman called Skeggi. However, another theory is that it comes from the Norse words for 'beard' and 'headland', and is a description of the way the headland here juts out into the sea, like a beard.

2. The North Sea was known as the German Ocean or German Sea until the early 20th century, when hostilities between Britain and Germany made the name unpopular.

3. The nature reserve a few miles south of Skegness is Gibraltar Point National Nature Reserve, with a wide variety of habitats – seashore, sand dunes, saltmarsh and freshwater marsh, ponds and lagoons. It is a key insect site, and rare species found there include many uncommon moths, several Red Data beetles, the Raft Spider and twelve species of dragonfly. The reserve is also particularly rich in birdlife, mostly wildfowl, waders and gulls, with an important breeding colony of Little Terns.

4. Skegness is sometimes referred to as 'the Blackpool of the East Coast', 'Nottingham by the Sea' (a reference to its popularity with holidaymakers from the Midlands, particularly from Nottingham), Costa del Skeg or Skegvegas.

5. The 'No Waiting' sign in Lumley Road in photograph S134062 (page 45) was used during the 'unilateral waiting' period in the early 1950s, when vehicles could wait on one side of the road on odd days of the month and on the opposite side on even days. The signs were hinged in half moons so that they could be tipped over to show which side of the road was currently available for parking.

6. The annual SkegX exhibition at the Embassy Theatre is the world's premier exhibition of Meccano creations. Hundreds of Meccano enthusiasts come to town to show off their exhibits, many of which are working models.

7. The 'Lincolnshire Poacher' is an all-weather Mersey class lifeboat, one of Skegness's two lifeboats at the RNLI station.

8. Bob, a Lincolnshire-built Hornsby traction engine, is one of the exhibits at Church Farm Museum at Church Road South.

9. On 1st April 2009 the 'Skegness Standard' ran a story that the town's famous landmark of the Jubilee Clock Tower at the end of Lumley Road was going to be dismantled and taken to a museum.

10. The Battle of Granny's Opening took place in 1908. Most of the land on the North Shore Estate had come into the possession of Laurence Kirk, a Nottingham solicitor. After building houses on the town end of the land, he decided to use the northern section for a second golf links for the town (the Seacroft Links had opened some years earlier). Kirk's land was bisected by what was claimed to be a public footpath, which ran from Roman Bank through the dunes to the seashore at a point called Granny's Opening and was a main access for the people of Winthorpe. Without consultation, Kirk blocked the pathway at both ends with stout posts and barbed wire, a most unpopular move amongst the people living on that part of Roman Bank and in Church Lane, one of whom was Samuel Moody, a town councillor. Samuel Moody roused the Winthorpers for battle, and on 18th May 1908, armed with axes, pitchforks and wire snippers, the eager troops stormed the barricades and made short work of the hated obstruction. An irate Mr Kirk summoned the ringleaders for trespass and malicious damage. The hearing took place at Spilsby Sessons House, and a large number of supporters travelled from Skegness, packing the courtroom to capacity. The main argument centred on the right of way problem; witnesses for the defence deposed that the footpath had been used for more than 60 years without hindrance, while plaintiffs claimed that 'Private' notices had once been positioned at the entrances. When all had had their say, the chairman of the bench announced that a right of way had been proved, and that the footpath must be restored to its original form. Kirk appealed to the Quarter Sessions at Lincoln, but the judgement was upheld and Granny's Opening remains a well-used footpath across the North Shore Links to this day.

Did You Know?
SKEGNESS
A MISCELLANY

SKEGNESS, THE CLOCK TOWER 1910 62848

Did You Know?
SKEGNESS
A MISCELLANY

FRANCIS FRITH

PIONEER VICTORIAN PHOTOGRAPHER

Francis Frith, founder of the world-famous photographic archive, was a complex and multi-talented man. A devout Quaker and a highly successful Victorian businessman, he was philosophical by nature and pioneering in outlook. By 1855 he had already established a wholesale grocery business in Liverpool, and sold it for the astonishing sum of £200,000, which is the equivalent today of over £15,000,000. Now in his thirties, and captivated by the new science of photography, Frith set out on a series of pioneering journeys up the Nile and to the Near East.

INTRIGUE AND EXPLORATION

He was the first photographer to venture beyond the sixth cataract of the Nile. Africa was still the mysterious 'Dark Continent', and Stanley and Livingstone's historic meeting was a decade into the future. The conditions for picture taking confound belief. He laboured for hours in his wicker dark-room in the sweltering heat of the desert, while the volatile chemicals fizzed dangerously in their trays. Back in London he exhibited his photographs and was 'rapturously cheered' by members of the Royal Society. His reputation as a photographer was made overnight.

VENTURE OF A LIFE-TIME

By the 1870s the railways had threaded their way across the country, and Bank Holidays and half-day Saturdays had been made obligatory by Act of Parliament. All of a sudden the working man and his family were able to enjoy days out, take holidays, and see a little more of the world.

With typical business acumen, Francis Frith foresaw that these new tourists would enjoy having souvenirs to commemorate their days out. For the next thirty years he travelled the country by train and by pony and trap, producing fine photographs of seaside resorts and beauty spots that were keenly bought by millions of Victorians. These prints were painstakingly pasted into family albums and pored over during the dark nights of winter, rekindling precious memories of summer excursions. Frith's studio was soon supplying retail shops all over the country, and by 1890 F Frith & Co had become the greatest specialist photographic publishing company in the world, with over 2,000 sales outlets, and pioneered the picture postcard.

FRANCIS FRITH'S LEGACY

Francis Frith had died in 1898 at his villa in Cannes, his great project still growing. By 1970 the archive he created contained over a third of a million pictures showing 7,000 British towns and villages.

Frith's legacy to us today is of immense significance and value, for the magnificent archive of evocative photographs he created provides a unique record of change in the cities, towns and villages throughout Britain over a century and more. Frith and his fellow studio photographers revisited locations many times down the years to update their views, compiling for us an enthralling and colourful pageant of British life and character.

We are fortunate that Frith was dedicated to recording the minutiae of everyday life. For it is this sheer wealth of visual data, the painstaking chronicle of changes in dress, transport, street layouts, buildings, housing and landscape that captivates us so much today, offering us a powerful link with the past and with the lives of our ancestors.

Computers have now made it possible for Frith's many thousands of images to be accessed almost instantly. The archive offers every one of us an opportunity to examine the places where we and our families have lived and worked down the years. Its images, depicting our shared past, are now bringing pleasure and enlightenment to millions around the world a century and more after his death.

For further information visit: www.francisfrith.com

INTERIOR DECORATION

Frith's photographs can be seen framed and as giant wall murals in thousands of pubs, restaurants, hotels, banks, retail stores and other public buildings throughout Britain. These provide interesting and attractive décor, generating strong local interest and acting as a powerful reminder of gentler days in our increasingly busy and frenetic world.

FRITH PRODUCTS

All Frith photographs are available as prints and posters in a variety of different sizes and styles. In the UK we also offer a range of other gift and stationery products illustrated with Frith photographs, although many of these are not available for delivery outside the UK – see our web site for more information on the products available for delivery in your country.

THE INTERNET

Over 100,000 photographs of Britain can be viewed and purchased on the Frith web site. The web site also includes memories and reminiscences contributed by our customers, who have personal knowledge of localities and of the people and properties depicted in Frith photographs. If you wish to learn more about a specific town or village you may find these reminiscences fascinating to browse. Why not add your own comments if you think they would be of interest to others? See **www.francisfrith.com**

PLEASE HELP US BRING FRITH'S PHOTOGRAPHS TO LIFE

Our authors do their best to recount the history of the places they write about. They give insights into how particular towns and villages developed, they describe the architecture of streets and buildings, and they discuss the lives of famous people who lived there. But however knowledgeable our authors are, the story they tell is necessarily incomplete.

Frith's photographs are so much more than plain historical documents. They are living proofs of the flow of human life down the generations. They show real people at real moments in history; and each of those people is the son or daughter of someone, the brother or sister, aunt or uncle, grandfather or grandmother of someone else. All of them lived, worked and played in the streets depicted in Frith's photographs.

We would be grateful if you would give us your insights into the places shown in our photographs: the streets and buildings, the shops, businesses and industries. Post your memories of life in those streets on the Frith website: what it was like growing up there, who ran the local shop and what shopping was like years ago; if your workplace is shown tell us about your working day and what the building is used for now. Read other visitors' memories and reconnect with your shared local history and heritage. With your help more and more Frith photographs can be brought to life, and vital memories preserved for posterity, and for the benefit of historians in the future.

Wherever possible, we will try to include some of your comments in future editions of our books. Moreover, if you spot errors in dates, titles or other facts, please let us know, because our archive records are not always completely accurate—they rely on 140 years of human endeavour and hand-compiled records. You can email us using the contact form on the website.

Thank you!

For further information, trade, or author enquiries please contact us at the address below:

The Francis Frith Collection, Frith's Barn, Teffont, Salisbury, Wiltshire, England SP3 5QP.

Tel: +44 (0)1722 716 376 Fax: +44 (0)1722 716 881
e-mail: sales@francisfrith.co.uk **www.francisfrith.com**